Valliant, Doris
Personal Finance
33879

332
V4
C-

DATE DUE

Nov 2, 2007	

PRINTED IN U.S.A.

EXPLORING
BUSINESS
AND
ECONOMICS

MONEY AND BANKING

FAMOUS FINANCIERS AND INNOVATORS

WORLD TRADE

THE STOCK MARKET

TAXES

THE ECONOMY

INVESTING YOUR MONEY

PERSONAL FINANCE

EXPLORING
BUSINESS
AND
ECONOMICS

Personal
Finance

Doris Valliant

Chelsea House Publishers
Philadelphia

Frontis: Saving pennies adds up; school children from Staten Island, New York, sort over $3,000 worth of pennies they collected for charity.

CHELSEA HOUSE PUBLISHERS

EDITOR-IN-CHIEF Sally Cheney
DIRECTOR OF PRODUCTION Kim Shinners
PRODUCTION MANAGER Pamela Loos
ART DIRECTOR Sara Davis

Choptank Syndicate/Chestnut Productions

EDITORIAL Norman Macht and Mary Hull
PRODUCTION Lisa Hochstein
PICTURE RESEARCH Norman Macht

http://www.chelseahouse.com

First Printing

1 3 5 7 9 8 6 4 2

Library of Congress Cataloging-in-Publication Data

Valliant, Doris.
     Personal Finance / Doris Valliant.
     p. cm. – (Exploring business and economics)
     ISBN 0-7910-6642-8 (alk. paper)
1. Finance, Personal. I. Title. II. Series.

     HG179 .V327 2001
     332.024—dc21

                                        2001042510

Table of Contents

1   Why Manage Your Money?   7

2   What Is a Budget?   15

3   Saving Your Money   25

4   Using a Bank   35

5   What Is Credit?   47

    Glossary   60

    Further Reading   62

    Index   63

The best way to save your money is to put some of it away before you go to a store and see all the tempting things you'd like to buy.

Why Manage Your Money

You finally convince your parents to give you an allowance. Five dollars every week handed to you for taking out the trash and emptying the dishwasher. You also have the opportunity to earn extra cash for seasonal chores like raking leaves or shoveling snow. With your allowance you can buy toys, video games, and snacks.

A week later you've discovered how fast your money can disappear. That five dollar bill you received on Saturday lasted only till Monday afternoon, when you spent the last 50 cents on a candy bar. Where did your money go? How can you stretch those dollars?

Spending money wisely takes planning and discipline. This book is a guide to teach you how to organize your **finances** and control your spending habits. Personal finance management involves setting up a **budget,** then following that plan. It involves living within or even below your means and saving. Sound personal finance is not giving in to impulses that zap your cash flow and reinforce bad spending habits. Building good money habits is a lifelong skill that pays huge dividends.

Sam Walton, the founder of Wal-Mart, a national chain of discount stores, learned sound financial habits at an early age. Walton redefined how retailers do business, and how we, the **consumers,** buy our goods and services. When he died in 1992, he was one of the world's richest and most respected businessmen. How did Sam Walton, an unpretentious man from Bentonville, Arkansas, achieve such astounding success?

Sam and his brother, Bud, grew up in the 1930s during the **Great Depression,** when jobs were scarce and money was hard to earn. Although Sam's parents had very little extra money, that didn't stop his father from saving some of the family **income,** and he taught this important lesson to his sons.

Sam and his brother helped contribute to the family finances rather than always taking money from their parents. They learned not to spend money carelessly, and when they did spend money, they used as little as possible, always finding the best bargains.

When Sam was seven years old, he began developing money management skills. He earned his first income selling magazine subscriptions. He started lifelong financial habits—budgeting, saving, and making wise choices about spending his money. By the seventh grade, he had

When Sam Walton was young, he learned how to earn and save money. Later he used those lessons to make Wal-Mart the largest retailer in the world.

a newspaper route that he continued until he graduated from college. During this time, he expanded his route, hired helpers, and turned it into a business that earned $4,000 to $5,000 annually—serious money in those times.

Sam used this income to pay for his clothes, college tuition, food, and fraternity expenses. His parents would have helped if they could, but they had no extra money for college. By the time Sam graduated from the University of Missouri, he had a strong work ethic and a deeply ingrained respect for the value of a dollar.

In 1950, when he opened Walton's, a variety store on the square in Bentonville, Arkansas, he planted the seed that eventually grew into Wal-Mart. Sam Walton managed his growing corporation by applying the personal financial skills he had learned as a boy.

Some businesses don't adopt successful financial practices. Profitable money management doesn't depend on how much money the company brings in, but on how well those earnings are handled. During the 1990s Internet companies sprouted up all over the information highway. Some flourished; many have gone out of business.

From September 1999 to October 2000, more than 117 Internet companies failed. Some went bankrupt and shut down their websites. Others made radical changes to their business practices, and a few had massive layoffs. These unprofitable companies followed business practices that didn't generate enough revenue, or the managers overspent. Internet companies that succeed will do so in part because they made prudent choices about expenses.

You're not a billionaire like Sam Walton or a struggling Internet company, but you want to manage your allowance so that it doesn't disappear faster than a snowball in July. It's not how much allowance you get; it's what you do with your money that's important.

What do financially successful people do with their money? They set up a personal financial plan, establish goals, and save part of their income. A budget is the first part of that plan. A budget means you'll get more out of the money you spend. It can help you to pay your bills and to achieve your goals. It also shows you where your money has gone.

What if you want an expensive video game system or a new bike, but your parents say they can't afford it? You save the money. Saving can be accomplished in many ways. You can put money away in your sock drawer or a piggy bank, or open a savings account at your local **bank.** You'll discover that banks offer several ways to save.

You could ask your parents to charge your new game equipment on their **credit card.** Charging doesn't take cash out of their pockets. Or does it? Using credit cards enables us to purchase products at warp speed. Unfortunately, the bills these cards generate may take years to pay off, and they cost your parents additional money in **interest** charges—costs associated with borrowing money from credit card companies.

When you gain control over your money, you take charge of a big part of your life. Wise money management can improve how you live. Spend responsibly, and you can live well on a small income and save money, too. On the other hand, poor financial habits can get you into serious trouble, no matter how much income you have. Little debts not dealt with grow into big debts that can take over your life.

Quotable Finance

"It requires a great deal of boldness and a great deal of caution to make a great fortune, and when you have it, it requires ten times as much skill to keep it."
— Ralph Waldo Emerson

"Beware of little expenses; a small leak will sink a great ship."
— Benjamin Franklin

"He who does not economize will have to agonize."
— Confucius

"Lack of money is no obstacle. Lack of an idea is an obstacle."
— Ken Hakuta

Pets.com, which produced these doggy sock puppets, was one of many new Internet businesses that failed in 2000 due to stiff competition and the lack of a solid business plan.

Setting financial goals and sticking to them will keep the debt monster under control. Sam Walton learned these principles as a boy: when you adhere to your objectives, they become realities; people with goals usually reach them; people without goals, don't.

Money-smart people are goal setters. They avoid wasteful spending by carefully planning where their money goes, and they follow their plans. Sometimes they have to make adjustments to this plan, but they never stop setting priorities.

For better or worse, money is connected to many parts of our lives. Money cannot buy happiness, but it does help us acquire some of life's necessities and a few of its luxuries. Money can also help provide the freedom to make choices. Successful personal finance means managing your income, no matter how large or small, to meet your obligations and to accomplish your goals.

Running a neighborhood lemonade stand is one of the most popular summer money makers for kids. Nine-year-old Tyler Logwood of Columbia, Missouri, said he made $17 selling lemonade, and planned to put the money toward a miniature radio or TV.

What Is a Budget?

Financial experts suggest that the number one requirement to build wealth is to make a budget, then stick to it. A budget is a plan that helps you establish spending goals and keeps track of how well you meet them. A budget sets a limit on how much you will spend on a given item. Your budget can help you achieve a particular goal, or encourage you to spend within your income. With a budget, you're in control of your money, and you quickly see how you have spent it.

Following a sound financial plan means spending less than you earn. A budget helps you do this. Most people don't know where their money goes until they track their expenses.

Find an old spiral notebook that you never filled up—don't waste your allowance on a new one. For one week, use it to keep track of how you spend your money. Write down every cent you pay out and what you spent it for. Every penny. Pull that notebook out of your backpack even when you think it's too much trouble to write it down every time you hand over some change. Do it anyway.

At the end of the week you'll be amazed to discover where your money went. You'll see a pattern in the record that tells you something about yourself. How much did you spend on impulse? What purchases were necessities? What could you live without or spend less on?

Once you've seen where your money goes, you can budget realistically. A budget is a way to control urges to spend. It helps you live within your income, by setting a

Quotable Finance

"The only reason not to budget is that you're so rich you can buy everything you want and still have money left over. If you don't fit this description, you need a budget."
— Jane Bryant Quinn

"It is not how much one makes but to what purpose one spends."
— John Ruskin

"If money is your hope for independence you will never have it. The only real security that a man will have in this world is a reserve of knowledge, experience, and ability."
— Henry Ford

"We first make our habits, and then our habits make us."
— John Dryden

George Washington was a farmer before he was a soldier and president. He kept detailed books showing his income and expenses at Mount Vernon. Thomas Jefferson, also a farmer, kept a ledger of everything he spent.

limit on how much you'll spend for any one kind of thing. Most important, budgeting makes you think about your choices and your values—what matters to you. A budgeting habit will support your goals for a lifetime.

That's how Sam Walton built his wealth. He learned budgeting habits when he was growing up and followed them for the rest of his life. He applied the same sound financial practices (in larger form) to his business.

A budget must be flexible in order to succeed. If you make your budget uncomplicated and informal, it will be easier to live with. However, you must be realistic about

Many people save pennies in huge jars. At times shortages result and the United States Mint has to increase its penny production. As prices rise, some people argue that pennies should be eliminated.

your income and expenses. Before you list your income and expenses, consider your financial goals and your personal needs. What you believe to be your goals and needs today could change, so be prepared to revise your plan at any time.

First, list all your income. Make your budgetary categories specific and not too broad. List all your sources of money: allowance, extra earnings, awards, interest on savings. Don't forget any cash gifts you may have received for your birthday or as a Christmas or Hannukah present. Next, enter your planned expenditures. Be specific. For example, instead of entertainment, break that category down into CDs, movies, videos, video games, or any other forms of entertainment. Other expenditures may include jewelry, gifts, and meals you eat out at the mall food court or neighborhood hot dog stand.

As you record your expenses, remember that you spend your money in two ways. Some items you buy are necessities, such as lunch or school supplies. These necessities are called **nondiscretionary** items. You need them. (You could go without lunch to buy something you want; that's a choice you make.) In your parents' budget, nondiscretionary expenses might include food, transportation, housing, utilities, phone, insurance, taxes, loan repayments, and any other obligation they must meet.

Discretionary spending is the second way we use our money. These are things we want, but don't need. Snacks, sports cards, movies, and video games are discretionary expenses. You don't really need them, but you sure do want them. In your parents' budget, discretionary items may include vacations, eating out, and entertainment.

When you tracked your money, how many times did you write down purchases that were made on impulse? How many purchases were for something you wanted but didn't really need? Probably the record of discretionary purchases is longer than the nondiscretionary list. Discretionary items creep up on us and snatch our money away before we realize that it's gone.

One way to gain control of discretionary spending is to set a goal for saving money. Writing an expense down makes it real and easier to remember when you have to choose between wants and needs. Decide what's most important to you. If your goal is to save enough money to afford a $350 bicycle, giving up some other things will feel less like a

Washington's Pennies

George Washington kept track of every penny spent on farm and household implements for his home, Mount Vernon. This wise money management turned Mount Vernon into a thriving, profitable plantation.

sacrifice as the money accumulates in savings, and you come closer to reaching your goal.

Make a list of your needs and your wants. Then set your priorities. Be flexible, because what you think you must buy today may not mean so much to you a month from now.

Keep your accounts in whatever way it suits you. The action of budgeting is more important than the form your budget takes. Just be sure you record your income and expenses. You might create a chart with categories for Weekly Income (allowance, extra money for chores, outside job, cash, gifts) and Expenses (saving for a CD or new bike, spending for lunch, sports cards, school supplies).

If you want to see where your money goes, get out some envelopes, folders, plastic containers, or empty jars. Inside these containers place the money you want to set aside, or write on a slip of paper the amount you are allocating. Another way to set up a budget is to use computer programs like Intuit's Quicken or Microsoft's Money. Whether you design a high-tech spreadsheet or use jars and envelopes doesn't matter. Just choose the system that works best for you and stick with your plan.

A budget works only if you follow it. Money management experts advise that a good budget must be well planned, practical, flexible, and easy to understand. However, keep in mind that a budget is a guide, not a ruler. Follow this guide for six months; then look for any adjustments you need to make. By then you'll know where your money goes. Any time your financial conditions change, adjust your budget. A budget is a dynamic document that requires periodic modification.

Always pay yourself first. Put aside what you want to save. Then **allocate** the rest of your income to your expenses. Never wipe out things that make you the happiest. You still

There are many odd jobs to do to increase your income. One way to earn extra money is by walking dogs for your neighbors, especially if they don't have time to do it themselves.

need to laugh sometimes. Fun is an essential force in life, but not the only force. If you don't get some fun out of your money, you'll crumple your budget plan into a ball and toss it into the trash.

One way to find fun money is to reduce your expenses. Don't slash and burn. Squeeze gently but firmly from one or more budget categories until you find that extra cash. If you slash a category, it will sprout up somewhere else. Don't kid yourself—you still want those video games or other discretionary items.

Put your budget in a visible place where you can check your progress or be reminded to live within your means. If you hide your budget away in a drawer, it can't help you. Hang a bulletin board in your room and tack your budget on it. Or tape it to your bedroom mirror. This way you get a daily reminder to spend wisely.

It's easy to increase expenses. But how can you increase your income? There are more ways to earn money than babysitting, paper routes, and mowing the lawn, although these are reliable options.

One way to make money is to find a need and fill that need with a skill you have. If you're a math whiz, maybe you can tutor other students who struggle with math, or tutor any other subject in which you excel. If you know how to use a computer, you can offer your computer services to others. (The adults in your family may become your best customers.) The next step is to make a flyer that explains the service you're offering and the fees you charge. Pass the flyers out in your neighborhood, and post them on community bulletin boards. Other ways to earn money are dog walking, window washing, housecleaning, or watering plants for your neighbors while they are on vacation. You could even set up a lemonade stand on a hot day and sell drinks. Your parents may be able to suggest some more alternatives. Always remember to check with your parents before pursuing these or any other money-making ideas

A budget is part of a sound financial plan, which should be shaped by your needs, wants, and goals. Financially successful people have a budget that includes goals and objectives, and they routinely save 10 percent of their income.

A budget should be simple, and it should set realistic goals. Your budget can be low or high tech, but it will work only if you honor it on a daily basis.

When you deposit money into a savings account, whether you use an ATM or a bank teller, you earn more money because the bank pays you interest on your savings.

Saving Your Money

How can you make your money grow? You can't plant dollar bills in the ground and hope they'll sprout into huge money trees. But you can open a savings account at your local bank, or use that piggy bank hidden in your closet. If you don't have a piggy bank, find a transparent jar—a big one.

Saving is whatever portion of our income we leave unspent. Americans don't save much. We rank 16th out of 24 western countries. But you don't have to be part of this dismal statistic.

Remember the first rule of budgeting: pay yourself first. If you don't, no one else will. Putting yourself first means reserving part of your income each week and adding it to your savings.

For example, if you get $5 weekly allowance, drop 25 or 50 cents in your jar every week. Those quarters will quickly add up. Adding additional money to your jar instead of spending it will help it multiply faster. When that jar gets full, roll those coins, and deposit them in your bank savings account.

Saving, like budgeting, is another lifetime habit that pays huge dividends. Decide what is an appropriate percentage of your income to reserve, and do it. Apply the remaining money to your expenses. Financially successful people routinely budget and save 10 percent of their income. This might be stretching your allowance tighter than you can stand, but 5 percent is always manageable, even on a meager allowance.

In fact, you don't need to accumulate huge chunks of money to reap big rewards. Those quarters will fill up your jar if you regularly drop them inside. If you wait to stock-pile big chunks of money, like 5 and 10 dollars at a time, you may not be as successful. Haphazardly putting away larger amounts will not teach you the important practice of saving. You want to make saving a lifetime habit. The consistency of storing away those weekly quarters develops this routine.

The Education IRA

Ask your parents to investigate this important way to save money for your college. An Education IRA allows your parents to save up to $500 a year toward college. The interest on this type of IRA is not taxable if it is used to pay for college expenses

A U.S. savings bond is an IOU from the federal government, which promises to repay you the amount of the loan, plus interest. This $1,000 U.S. savings bond featuring Albert Einstein was introduced in 1998.

Sometimes you will be saving for specific goals. These goals can be modest—something you can achieve in a few weeks, or within a month. If you are saving for a particular item, such as a mountain bike or a video game, paste a picture of a bike or the game on your jar. If you are depositing your money in the bank, design a chart around your picture. Charting your progress and seeing your goal will help you achieve it.

Don't beat up on yourself if you miss a weekly deposit in your savings account. Sometimes our impulses overcome our good judgment. Just resume your regular saving routine. Remind yourself that the money you wasted on an impulsive purchase won't be as gratifying to you as that new bike or video game, which you'll enjoy for a long time.

If you are accumulating funds for an expensive item, you may want to consider earning interest on your savings. Opening a savings account at your local bank is the smartest way. A bank savings account is a **deposit** account that earns interest on the money put into it. Interest is money the bank pays you for allowing it to use your money. Every month or quarter the bank sends you a statement, a printed record that shows all deposits and earned interest in your account. Some banks offer special accounts that combine checking and savings transactions into one monthly statement.

Many banks offer holiday savings clubs. These accounts require you to deposit a fixed sum of money every week so that you will build up the desired amount in time for holiday spending. You can make the deposit yourself or transfer the amount from your regular savings account. Holiday savings clubs are good ideas if they pay as high an interest as your savings account, but some holiday savings clubs pay no interest. These are not a good investment of your money.

Other savings plans include: **money market accounts**, **Individual Retirement Accounts (IRAs),** and **certificates of deposit (CDs).** These are three different ways to get your money to grow.

Money market accounts pay higher interest than regular savings accounts, but they may require a minimum deposit and maintenance of a minimum **balance.** A balance is the amount of money in the account at any given time. Money market accounts allow you to write a certain number of checks each month, but you cannot let your balance fall below the minimum amount required. Some money market accounts will not let you write a check for less than $100.

An IRA helps your parents prepare for their retirement. They can open an IRA at any time in their working years, the earlier the better. The government doesn't tax the interest your parents earn on an IRA until after they retire. Although they still have to pay taxes, these taxes are usually lower than when they were working.

Bank teller Stephanie Dulin helps Ryan Tarr deposit money in his savings account at the Talbot Bank of Easton, Maryland. Ryan's savings will earn him more money as the bank pays him interest on his savings.

One other type of savings account is a certificate of deposit (CD). Like savings and money market accounts, CDs earn interest. A CD pays a guaranteed interest rate because the bank knows it will have your money for a set period of time.

CDs have advantages and disadvantages. CDs require a minimum investment, usually at least $500, but some banks offer ones for $250, for a fixed length of time. If you withdraw the money before the CD matures, you may pay a penalty and lose a considerable amount of interest. You must be sure that you won't need the money before the CD comes due.

The advantage of a CD is that you can't get to this money and spend it. CDs earn higher interest than regular savings accounts and money market accounts. CDs give you

Personal Savings

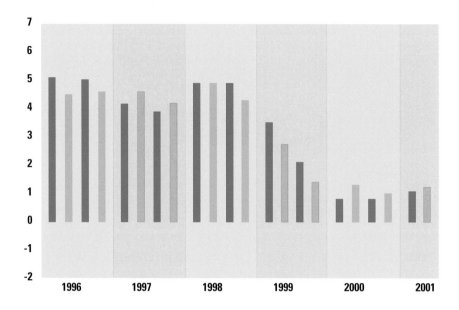

According to the Bureau of Economic Analysis, Americans have been saving less money in the last 10 years. As savings shrink, banks have less money to lend to home buyers and businesses, and people have less money in reserve in case they lose their jobs or emergencies occur in their lives.

choices about how long your money is tied up. You can buy a CD for as short a time as 30 days and for as long as five years. Some CDs offer **compounded** interest.

Interest—the money a bank pays you for allowing it to use your money—is the magic fertilizer that makes your money grow. The bank takes the money you deposit into your savings account or CD and lends it to someone else. Banks set varying interest rates for different accounts and balances. Money market accounts and certificates of deposit offer the best rates. Each interest rate is a percentage that is compounded and added to your savings balance.

Compounding makes your money grow because you earn interest not just on the dollars you deposit, but also on the interest itself.

Most savings accounts pay compounded interest in one of two ways. Day-of-deposit to day-of-withdrawal usually gives you more because all the money in your account earns money every day it's there. Average daily balance means that the bank figures interest only on the average balance in the account for each day in the period.

Here's how compound interest works. Suppose you deposit $1,000 in a savings account that pays six percent simple interest per year. At the end of one year, your $1,000 has grown to $1,060. Now suppose you deposit the same $1,000 in an account at six percent interest, compounded monthly. At the end of the first month, you will have earned $1/12$ of six percent: $5.00. After the second month the interest added to your account is $5.03. At the end of one year your $1,000 will have become almost $1,072.

Another way to make your money grow is to invest in **U. S. savings bonds.** The government pays you interest

The Rule of 72

The Rule of 72 shows how many years it will take for your savings to double. For example, if you deposit $100 in an eight percent savings bond it will take nine years to grow to $200. That's 72 divided by 8 equals 9. In a regular bank savings account earning three percent interest the same $100 will take 24 years to reach $200. Maybe you'd rather buy a government savings bond the next time you go to the bank.

for allowing them to use your money. For as little as $25, you can buy a savings bond that pays a guaranteed interest rate for up to 30 years. The first U.S. savings bonds were Liberty Loans, a fund-raising drive during World War I to help pay for the war effort. From 1939 to 1945 the United States government issued Series E bonds to finance World

The Magic of Compounding

The magic of compounding may be illustrated by starting with a penny. Put the penny on a table. The next day, add another penny. Now there are two. Add two more pennies. Every day double the number of pennies that are already on the table.

After two weeks you will have saved $81.92. After four weeks you will be a millionaire.

Day	Amount	Day	Amount
1	$0.01	16	$327.68
2	$0.02	17	$655.34
3	$0.04	18	$1,310.72
4	$0.08	19	$2,621.44
5	$0.16	20	$5,242.88
6	$0.32	21	$10,485.76
7	$0.64	22	$20,971.52
8	$1.28	23	$41,943.04
9	$2.56	24	$83,886.08
10	$5.12	25	$167,772.16
11	$10.24	26	$335,544.32
12	$20.48	27	$671,088.64
13	$40.96	28	$1,342,177.28
14	$81.92	29	$2,684,354.56
15	$163.84	30	$5,368,709.12

War II and control inflation. Series E bonds were so popular that the government sold $54 billion worth of them during and after the war.

If you have trouble holding on to money, U. S. savings bonds may be a workable solution for you. Like certificates of deposit, bonds lock away your money. However, you can cash in the bond without penalty six months after you purchase it. Of course, the longer you let the government keep your money, the more interest you earn. The interest is added monthly and compounded semiannually. You can purchase saving bonds at banks, or you can buy them online at www.savingsbonds.gov.

Saving involves that part of your income you don't spend. Always remember to save before you spend. You can open a bank savings account, buy a certificate of deposit, or purchase a U.S. savings bond. When you use any of these savings plans, your money will grow because it earns interest.

Whatever way you choose to save your money, make setting aside part of your income—5 or 10 percent if you can—a habit as ingrained as brushing your teeth every day. Adhering to this all-important financial practice means you are in charge of your money instead of having your emotions and money controlling you.

THE PATH OF A CHECK

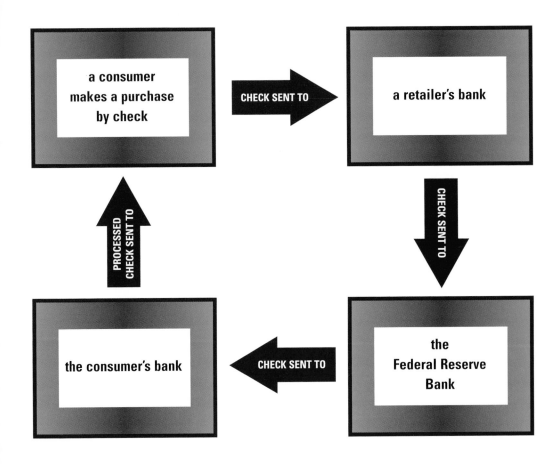

This is what happens when a customer writes a check to pay a bill or buy something. The check becomes money in the seller's account and the amount is subtracted from the account of the person who wrote the check.

Using a Bank

Ever since you set up your budget, you've worked hard to change your spending habits and increase your income. You've earned money helping your neighbors with various jobs. In addition, your mom and dad have paid you for extra chores that aren't part of your allowance. Suddenly the shoebox crammed with all this extra cash is about to burst. Where can you safely store all these dollars and still have easy access when you need some money?

Your parents suggest that you open a checking account at their bank. Because you are under 18 years of age, your dad or mom must open the account in his or her name, with your name underneath. This type of account is called a custodial account. Even though the account is for you, your parents or a guardian are in charge of it until you turn 18; then the account is yours.

When you set up this new account, you fill out several forms. One of the most important forms is the signature card that you must sign. This card verifies that you are the person making **transactions** (depositing or withdrawing money) on your account. The bank teller may check the signature on a banking transaction against the one on your signature card. If you are cashing a check—withdrawing money from your account—the bank teller wants to make sure she is giving the money to you, the owner of the checking account, and not some impostor.

A checking account means that the bank will hold the money you deposit into your account. A deposit adds money to your account or, in banking terms, is credited to the account. Be sure you are putting money in a bank that is insured by the **Federal Deposit Insurance Corporation (FDIC).** The FDIC, which is run by the U. S. government, guarantees to protect accounts up to $100,000. The FDIC also backs many money market accounts and certificates of deposits. Probably you'll never find enough extra chores to earn $100,000, but even if your account has only $100, the government promises to refund that $100 if the bank closes.

Now you can clean out your shoebox and take all those 5 and 10 dollar bills to the bank. At the bank, you fill out a deposit slip, hand it over to the bank teller with all your hard-earned cash, and the bank teller gives you a receipt for your money. This receipt is a carbon copy attached to the deposit ticket or an electronic receipt created when you make the deposit.

The deposit slip you wrote is printed with your name and address on it, along with the checking account number. When you opened your checking account, you ordered these personalized checks and deposit slips. To ensure against bank errors, always use these printed documents when you are making a bank transaction.

With your money in a checking account, you no longer have to worry about your brother borrowing from your shoebox, or about dollar bills falling over the side of the box and disappearing. Getting money out of the bank is as easy as dipping your hand into the box.

When you write a check, you withdraw money from your account. This **withdrawal** is subtracted from your balance, or in banking terms, **debited** from your account. Your checking account balance works like your savings account balance; it tells you the amount of money you have to spend. Keep track of these withdrawals in your **check register**, so you know your account balance at all times.

The check register is in front of your checks. You record all deposits and withdrawals in it. Keeping an accurate check register is a very important step in managing your money. Every time you write a check, you list the name of the person or company, called the **payee,** to whom you wrote the check and the amount of the check. Then you subtract the amount of the check from the account balance.

For example, suppose you opened your checking account with $100, which is the beginning balance. This amount appears at the beginning of the check register. A week later you deposit $15 and enter that figure under "Deposits" in your check register. Now your record shows a balance of $115, because you added the $15 to the original $100.

Later that week you discover Movietime Videos has a sale on video games. You write them a $10 check for a game.

In your register, you enter the payee, Movietime Videos, and under "Withdrawals" you write $10. Then you subtract the $10 from $115, and write in the new $105 balance.

A check is a substitute for cash. The check promises the payee, such as Movietime Videos, that your bank account has enough money to pay out the amount on the check. That is why keeping an up-to-date check register is so crucial, so that you know your balance.

If you intentionally write a check for more than the balance in your account, you are breaking the law. If you have $100 in your account, and you write a check for $150, you have written a "bad check." It won't take very long for the bank and stores to discover that you are writing bad checks. They'll contact the police who will be knocking on your door with their handcuffs ready.

Sometimes we think we have plenty of money in our checking accounts, but we don't. Unintentionally writing a check for more than the balance is called "bouncing" a check, or in banking terms, an **overdraft** on an account. Either way, your check bounces higher than a rubber ball and smacks your pocketbook with bank service fees.

Banks frown on bounced checks, even if you didn't mean to do it. That $150 check you wrote could cost you almost as much in service fees. The bank marks a bounced check "insufficient funds" and returns it to the store where you wrote it. You still are obligated for the merchandise you bought, and now you owe the bank additional money because your check was returned. Many banks levy a $20 or higher service charge for each bounced check. Businesses sometimes charge customers for bounced checks as well. Many stores post signs at the cash register which warn customers that $20 (or more) will be charged against them if their check is returned.

You pay an even higher fee personally. The store has lost faith in you as a reliable customer because that bad check labels you as untrustworthy and a financial risk. The next time you want to pay for merchandise with your personal check, the store may refuse your check if they suspect you do not have the funds in your checking account. Later on, when you want to establish **credit,** bounced checks may appear on your banking records when credit reporting agencies investigate your credit history.

In order to protect you from the embarrassment of unintentionally bouncing a check, the bank may offer you overdraft protection when you open your account. There is no charge for overdraft protection until you need it. If a check exceeds the funds in your checking account, the bank will honor your check, then automatically grant you a loan to cover the amount. Of course, this is a loan, which means in addition to settling the amount of the overdraft, you will pay the bank a fee for this service, plus interest on the money they lend you. To avoid these costly mistakes, wise money managers always keep track of all bank transactions in their check registers. This way they know exactly how much money they have.

The Origins of Banking

Modern banking began somewhere between 1200 and 1600 A.D. in Italy. The word bank comes from the Italian word *banco* or *banca,* meaning bench. In the street, early Italian bankers conducted their business on benches. Banking firms established their operations in Rome, Florence, and other Italian cities. Slowly, banking activities spread throughout Europe.

Way back in the 1500s a bank might consist of one person who borrowed money at one interest rate and loaned it to others at a higher interest rate.

Besides maintaining an accurate check register, it is important to make sure everything you write on a check is absolutely correct. Although a check acts like cash, it is a legal document. When you sign a check, you are guaranteeing that the bank will honor it and pay the amount to the person or business you wrote the check for. Before you complete the payee's name, you must date the check. To protect from fraud, write the amount not only in numbers, but also spell out the words completely and fill up any space left after the words with a long squiggly line. In this way no one can alter the amount you've written in figures and words. Always write checks in indelible ink so that no one can make any changes.

The last step in writing a check is to sign it. A check without your signature is invalid and will be returned to you to correct.

If someone gives you a check and you want to deposit it in your account, you must first endorse the check by signing your name on the back of the check. Since you are depositing this check rather than cashing it, you use a restrictive endorsement. Above your name you write "For Deposit Only," which restricts the bank from transferring the money into any account but yours.

Deposited checks are sent to central clearinghouses that sort them and deliver them to the banks they were drawn on. At the clearinghouse, a courier (messenger) from your bank collects the checks belonging to his bank. The courier leaves checks from the different financial institutions that his bank has received. Your check to Movietime Videos that was deposited into the store's account is now returned to your bank, where the $10 is deducted from your account. Every month you receive a bank statement that lists every transaction you made during that time period. On your current statement, you see the check number and $10 listed as a debit. This bank statement certifies that the $10 you paid to Movietime Videos has been honored, and the amount subtracted from your account.

When your bank statement arrives, compare the checks listed on the statement to the ones written in your check register. Any check recorded in the register but not shown on the statement is called an outstanding check because these checks have not been processed through the clearinghouse. You must subtract these outstanding checks from the balance shown on your bank statement so that you know exactly how much money is in your account. This procedure is called reconciling a bank statement; like keeping an accurate check register, it is an important step in successful money management.

Although banks continue to send printed statements each month, banking has joined the computer age. For many transactions today, financial institutions electronically transfer funds. Electronic banking allows customers with home computers to pay bills, check account balances, and transfer money between their accounts.

One of the most common electronic transactions is known as **direct deposit.** For many Americans, direct deposit is the way they get their paychecks. Employers direct the bank to transfer salary amounts from the company's account straight into each employee's account. Instead of holding a paper check in his hand, the employee gets a direct deposit receipt with all the payroll information. **Electronic fund transfers (EFTs)** are commonplace for many kinds of income, such as Social Security checks,

Write Checks Carefully

What happens if the numerals and words don't match on a check? The bank always goes by the written words. If the numbers are $19.95, but the words say "nineteen and no cents," the check will be cashed for $19.

Alexander Hamilton was America's first Secretary of the Treasury, in 1789. He believed in a strong central bank and promoted manufacturing to strengthen the national economy. Hamilton is considered the father of the modern banking system in the United States.

which the government deposits electronically into each recipient's account.

All deposits are credits to the accounts, so they are added to the account balance on the bank statement and in the check register. None of these electronic transactions—deposits or withdrawals—can occur unless the account holders give the bank authorization to withdraw funds or to deposit income into their checking or savings accounts.

The ATM or **automated teller machine** is probably the most familiar form of electronic banking. When your parents push a plastic card into the ATM, cash pops out like it is a magical money machine. Actually, that credit card look-alike is a debit card, which means every time it goes inside the ATM, the amount of money that comes out is subtracted from your parents' account. The ATM machine also allows cardholders to deposit money into their account.

A debit card takes the place of writing a check. It electronically transfers money from your bank account and puts it into the account of the person or store where you made a purchase.

ATMs provide access to our money 24 hours a day, 7 days a week, at locations from the local machines in our town to ATMs located in other states and countries. No matter where we are we can withdraw or deposit money, and receive information on our balance. Of course, we can't withdraw more money than we have in our accounts, and some banks limit the amount of ATM transactions.

Convenience can be costly. Banks often charge fees for ATMs. If you use the ATM owned by your bank, you may not have a fee; however, if you use an ATM that is not affiliated with your bank, you will pay a service fee that is charged against your account for each ATM transaction.

Many stores now take **debit cards,** which means the purchase is automatically debited from your account and credited to the stores. Carrying a debit card is a great convenience since you don't need a checkbook or lots of cash when you shop, and you are not increasing the balance on your MasterCard or Visa credit cards. Some banks charge a fee for this kind of transaction; others do not.

Most banks, savings and loan associations, and some credit unions issue debit cards. A **credit union** is a cooperative association made up of members who share a common bond, such as working for a large company or a non-profit corporation. For instance, your teachers probably belong to a local or statewide credit union that serves educational personnel. Credit unions operate like banks, but offer lower rates for loans and credit cards. A savings and loan association provides checking and savings accounts, money market accounts, IRAs, and makes business loans; however, its largest service is offering home **mortgages,** long-term loans used to purchase land or a house.

Banks vary in their size and the kinds of services they provide. The next time you drive through your town, notice the different financial institutions. Read the billboards advertising the services offered. Whether large or small, a full-service bank or a credit union, all are valuable resources for wise money managers.

Credit card companies often team up with businesses to offer cardholders special incentives to use their credit card. These cards allow holders to earn frequent flyer miles every time they use the card.

What Is Credit?

When you go shopping with your parents, how often do they pay for their purchases with a credit card? Have you ever asked them to use their credit card to pay for something you wanted—like a $100 Lego™ set? Every time they hand over that plastic card, they are really taking out a loan

The use of credit cards involves buying goods and services without paying for them at the time of the purchase. When shoppers buy on credit, they take out a loan. Credit cards are only one way we borrow money. Loans come in many forms, but they all mean that the **borrower** agrees to pay the lender over a period of time. When the borrower signs the loan agreement, he or she walks away with the product or service and promises to pay for it later. Delaying, or in financial terms, **deferring** payment sounds like a great idea, but it comes with a price.

Borrowers pay a finance charge, which is an amount of interest charged for the privilege of using a credit card or for dividing the purchase price into installment payments. This finance charge increases the cost because interest is added to the purchase price. Like the interest in your savings account, interest on a loan is stated as a percentage amount. But unlike your savings account, where the interest earns you money, loan interest is money you give to someone else. In other words, credit interest refers to money you are spending, not saving.

State governments put a ceiling on interest rates, which usually range from 18 to 22 percent, a high price to pay for the convenience of credit. Usury laws protect borrowers from unreasonably high rates beyond the state limits. Creditors who agree to lend money for high interest with a short repayment period are called loan sharks.

Loans and the interest charged on them can be repaid in installments or with a revolving line of credit. For many

The Cost of Credit

How expensive is maintaining a balance every month on a credit card? If the outstanding balance is $1,000, the interest charged is 18 percent, and you make a minimum payment of 2.5 percent every month, you'll pay off the $1000 in 7 years. It will cost you $730 in interest. So you will pay $1,730 to buy $1,000 worth of merchandise.

The problems caused by buying too much on credit are not new. People who run up too many debts by buying things they can't afford often wind up losing everything they have.

adults, buying a house, a car, an expensive appliance, or any other high-priced item involves setting up an installment payment plan. With installment payments, the buyer pays a set amount each month over a given period of time. This monthly payment includes the interest and part of the **principal,** which is the original price. The longer the borrower takes to repay the principal, the more interest he or she will pay.

The loan installment on a house is called a mortgage, and the monthly payments on a mortgage may run for as long as 30 years. Cars are usually paid for in monthly installments over three, four, or five years. When it's time for you to go to college, you may join millions of other students and their families who take out loans.

Car loans, mortgages, and many purchases that run in the hundreds of dollars are secured loans because the lender can repossess or take back the **collateral**—the television, the minivan, even a house—if the buyer fails to make the installment payments.

Defaulting on a loan may result in costly penalties as well as the loss of the merchandise and all the money paid on it.

The Dangers of Buying On Credit

When it comes time to go to college, be credit savvy. In 1996 the leading cause of 1.1 million personal bankruptcies was credit cards. College graduates filed many of these bankruptcies. As college students, they took out loans and used credit cards. Once they graduated, they struggled to make credit card payments, repay student loans, and cover their other living expenses. The following excerpt originally appeared in "Bob Levey's Washington" column in *The Washington Post*, May 7, 2000:

> About 11 years ago, I was eating dinner in a restaurant in Blacksburg, Virginia, home of Virginia Tech. My waiter happened to overhear me say that I worked for *The Washington Post*. He asked to talk to me once I was through eating. He told me that he had come to Tech as a student a year earlier, "a typical teenager with no experience in how the world really works." His parents had co-signed for a credit card for him. He was to use it only for emergencies. But very soon, the young man said, "I was the life of the party. I was picking up the tab for everyone, every night." Within three months, he had crashed out of school and had taken the waiter job. Two things were for sure, he told me.

Credit cards offer unsecured loans that give access to a fixed amount of money. The credit card company will not repossess what you buy, but there are equally nasty consequences if you default on a credit card bill.

Three major credit reporting bureaus—Equifax, TRW, and Trans-Union—keep track of the credit history for every person who takes out a loan or uses a credit card. When borrowers default on installment loans, and/or don't make at least the minimum payments on their credit card bills,

One, he was going to re-enroll at Tech as soon as he could. Two, he wouldn't have any credit cards once he did.

How common are such stories? Here are some numbers that will put a little curl in your hair: A survey by Teenage Research Unlimited found that 37 percent of 18- and 19-year-olds have credit cards in their own names. A survey done by Phoenix Home Life Insurance, of Hartford, Connecticut, found that 60 percent of American college students use credit cards, even though 20 percent can't explain the meaning of the phrase "buying on credit." The average balance carried by a credit-card-toting college student is $584, according to a publication called *Student Monitor.*

I'm not much for telling Capitol Hill what to do, but here goes with an idea that someone up there ought to run with: Make it illegal to obtain a credit card if you're under 21 unless you take a four-hour course in how to manage credit wisely. It would have saved the guy I met at Virginia Tech. "I just didn't know," he told me. "I ruined my life. I ruined my parent's trust in me. I'll never do it again. But I never would have done it at all if I'd known better."

A credit card seems like a magic wand to create money. But its overuse leaves trails of debts, not riches. Credit card salesmen appear on college campuses every year to sign up students. If you understand how credit cards work and the problems they can cause for you, you may save yourself some headaches.

that failure to pay goes on their credit report. Defaults are blemishes on their credit history that can scar their credit rating and create future problems.

People who have bad credit cannot hide this fact. Any prospective employer, retailer, bank, insurer, or any other approved recipient can request a credit report (for a fee). It is no secret when someone's credit rating plummets. A bad credit report affects your ability to obtain any type of loan, rent an apartment, or buy a house. Employers often check prospective employees' credit ratings before offering them a position.

Credit histories change quicker than the seasons. Updated information is fed constantly to the credit reporting bureaus. Too often Americans are making the unhappy discovery that their credit report is wrong.

Having an error on your credit report can be as damaging as actually defaulting on a loan. Old information that should have disappeared long ago may still show up and tarnish credit records. Even after borrowers call the credit reporting agency or write countless letters, these damaging comments continue to haunt their credit report. Sometimes these mistakes seem as permanent as the hieroglyphics on the Egyptian pyramids.

For many adults, going into debt has become a way of life. In the United States, about 80 percent of adults have credit cards, and most have a mortgage on their home. About 60 percent of college students (or their parents) take out loans to pay for college expenses. Some estimates conclude that most families average 12 credit cards and $8,000 of credit debt that may take six or more years to repay.

Managing credit is like keeping a two-headed dragon in your wallet. One head smiles and wants to help you. The other head blows fire and burns up your budget.

With credit, people pay for goods and services as part of their regular living expenses rather than having to wait until they can afford to make the purchase. Many of these purchases—like a house or a car—are so costly that saving up for them is nearly impossible. Many young people could not afford the high price of a college education without government and private college loans.

Credit cards simplify purchasing and bill paying. Consumers don't have to carry large sums of cash or their checkbook when they shop. Every month they write one check to cover all the merchandise and services bought during that time. Internet and catalog shoppers find the best way to order products is with a credit card.

Though credit cards can simplify our lives, they can also be dangerous. It is easy for shoppers to whip out that piece of plastic and forget that eventually they must pay the bill. Because consumers don't pull cash out of their wallets, credit cards allow them to buy more goods and services than they can afford. All those charges come due at the end of each month. Suddenly, their budget explodes with payments to several credit card companies on top of the mortgage, car loan, and other expenses.

Many consumers make only the minimum payment on the credit card bill instead of paying the balance in full. When credit card bills carry a balance from month to month, the cost of each item purchased dramatically increases, because the credit card issuer may be charging 18 percent interest or more on the remaining balance. On a $1000 balance, that's $15 a month interest. Paying your credit card balance in full each month will enable you to avoid all interest expenses. Credit is not free—for the consumer or the retailer. Every time customers buy merchandise on a credit card, the merchant hands the credit card company three percent or more of the sale.

Many banks and finance companies issue credit cards. But they are not all the same. Interest charges vary. For someone who intends to pay the bill in full each month, the interest rate doesn't matter. This person may prefer a card with the longest grace period, the time between when they are billed and when they have to pay. If the grace period is 25 days, the time period offered on many cards, they must pay the full balance within that time or the interest starts to

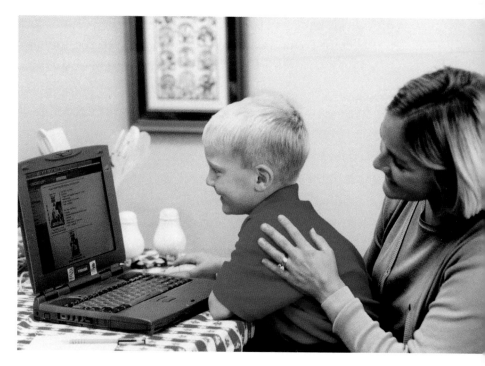

Internet and catalog shoppers use credit cards to make purchases online or over the telephone without ever having to leave home. This is convenient; it also makes it easier to overspend and end up owing more money than you can repay.

roll. Using the credit card company's money during the grace period is like getting an interest-free loan.

People who are likely to carry a balance from month to month need a card with the lowest interest rate possible. For people with good credit ratings, plenty of these cards exist. Credit unions usually offer the best deals, then banks. **Finance companies,** who are in the business of making all types of loans, usually charge the highest interest rates.

Competition among credit card companies is fierce, which keeps interest rates flexible. Many cards offer incentives—airplane frequent flyer miles for every purchase made on the card, or discounts on cars or other major products.

Some cards give full travel discounts and services, not just airplane miles. Phone companies are now in the credit card business, offering all kinds of deals combining credit and long distance service. Many of these deals seem too good to be true until customers realize they come with high fees or high interest charges.

The interest rate on a credit card is stated as the **annual percentage rate (APR).** The APR is figured on the size of the unpaid balance each month. If the APR on a credit card is 18 percent, every month 1.5 percent interest is added onto the unpaid balance. The quicker the balance is paid off, the less finance charges are incurred.

Interest, or APR rates, vary widely, depending on the type of credit offered, the borrower's credit history, and the amount of competition the creditor has in attracting new business. The financial institution that issues the credit card determines the APR. People with poor credit histories get credit cards, but they usually pay high interest rates because credit issuers fear they may default on the bill. Low APRs go to people with good credit histories, because they have an established record of paying their bills on time each month, even if they only make the minimum payments.

In addition to the APR, some cards have annual fees from $20 to $50. Some cards have no annual fee. Cardholders who pay their bill late or charge over their credit limit often face additional fees. Using services offered by the credit card, such as cash advances (which is like using an ATM, only you are borrowing money instead of withdrawing it from your account), also come with a fee attached.

If credit cards are lost, laws limit the amount of the cardholder's liability to $50 for each card. Issuing institutions often don't make customers pay even that much. Cardholders owe nothing for any charges provided they report the stolen or lost card within 60 days of the date of the statement on which the fraudulent charges appear.

The biggest credit card thieves are the cardholders themselves who overuse credit cards to spend beyond their incomes. This common pitfall robs their families of financial stability and heads them toward **bankruptcy.** When you become an adult, you can avoid drowning in credit card debt by paying cash for small things. Use credit wisely, always paying off the balance monthly. That way credit works for you. When applying for a loan, pay attention to the interest rate and the amount of time given to repay the loan. The longer you take to pay back the loan, the more money comes out of your pocket in interest charges.

Just as you tracked your spending by creating a budget, keep track of every credit card purchase. Save all your receipts. When your monthly statements arrive, check them carefully. Credit card companies do make mistakes. Protect your credit cards as you would cash in your wallet. Carry only cards you intend to use, and leave the others at home.

19th Century Credit: The Installment Plan

Although Isaac Singer, the inventor of the sewing machine, didn't have a Visa or MasterCard, he came up with the concept of buying on credit. In 1856, he offered to sell his sewing machines on the installment plan. For $5 down and $5 a month, families could buy a $125 machine and pay the cost over a period of time. Without buying on credit, the average family, with a typical annual income of $500, could not afford a sewing machine, one of many inventions that improved Americans' lives. Selling his sewing machines by the installment payment plan probably helped make Isaac Singer a very wealthy and successful man.

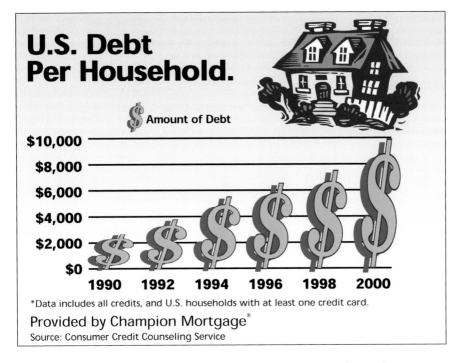

U.S. Debt Per Household.

$ Amount of Debt

*Data includes all credits, and U.S. households with at least one credit card.

Provided by Champion Mortgage®
Source: Consumer Credit Counseling Service

This graph illustrates how household debt in the United States has increased five-fold since 1990.

When you use a credit card, watch the clerk fill out the credit card slip. After you sign the slip, be sure you receive all the carbons. Tear up the carbons and throw them away so that no one can copy your credit card number. Make sure that the clerk hands you your card and not someone else's. Never give a credit card number to a phone solicitor. Only provide credit card information when you place a phone order.

Credit is good and bad. The choice is yours to make. If you buy goods and services on credit, while paying the minimum amount on each bill, then credit is like skating on a frozen pond and hearing the ice crack. Too many Americans with high-paying jobs are skating on financial thin ice, using credit to live beyond their means.

From 1992 to 1997, salaries rose about 5 percent a year, while consumer debt soared by 13 percent a year. Americans owe more than $1 trillion in revolving credit. Don't be lured into the credit card trap. Make credit work for you, not against you. Like budgeting and saving, the proper use of credit is another step toward sound personal finance.

Allocate—set aside for a purpose

Annual Percentage Rate (APR)—the interest rate on a credit card

Automated Teller Machine (ATM)—a computer terminal at banks, airports, shopping centers, and other locations where people can make deposits, transfer funds, and withdraw limited amounts of cash

Balance—the amount of money in a bank account; also the amount owed after part of the bill has been paid

Bank—a place of business for keeping, issuing, exchanging, and lending money

Bankruptcy—the financial condition of being unable to pay debts to individuals and businesses

Borrower—one who takes out a loan with the intention of repaying the amount

Budget—a spending plan that involves income and expenses

Certificate of deposit (CD)—a document issued by a financial institution for a special account that pays a higher rate of interest than a regular savings account, to earn this higher rate, a CD must be held over a certain amount of time

Check register—a ledger in which all deposits and withdrawls on a checking account are recorded

Collateral—a property pledged by the borrower as security for the loan, often the property is the item for which a loan has been made

Compound interest—interest computed on the principal and the interest earned

Consumer—one who purchases goods and services

Credit—time allowed for delayed payment of goods and services; also a term for money added to a bank account balance

Credit card—a card that identifies the holder and allows that person to charge the cost of goods and services from businesses

Credit union—a kind of bank formed by people who share a common bond; members pool their money for savings and loans

Debit—an amount of money subtracted from an account balance

Debit card—a card that subtracts a purchase cost directly from the holder's account

Default—failure to pay financial debts

Defer—to delay; put off

Deposit—to put money in a bank for safekeeping

Direct deposit—the electronic transfer of money directly between accounts

Discretionary—budgetary items that are variable and not considered necessities

Electronic funds transfers (EFT)—electronic transfer of money automatically from one account to another; an ATM is a type of EFT

FDIC—acronym for the Federal Deposit Insurance Corporation, which insures bank accounts up to $100,000 per account; many financial institutions are members of this government-backed corporation

Finance—the money or income a person has ready for use

Finance company—a business that loans money, usually at a high interest rate

Great Depression—a period during the 1930s when the American economy was in severe decline, leading to widespread poverty and unemployment

Income—money that comes in from property, business, or work

Interest—money paid for the use of money, usually a percentage of the amount borrowed or saved

IRA—acronym for an Individual Retirement Account, a retirement savings plan

Money market account—a type of savings account that usually pays a higher rate of interest than a regular savings account

Mortgage—a long-term loan to purchase land or a house

Nondiscretionary—budgetary items that are fixed expenses and usually necessities

Overdraft—when a check is drawn for more than the balance in an account

Payee—person to whom money is paid or to be paid

Principal—the amount borrowed or the amount that remains unpaid on a loan

Savings bonds—bonds sold to individuals by the U.S. government that earn interest over a specified amount of time

Transaction—term used to describe the process of depositing or withdrawing money from a bank, credit union, or other financial institution

Withdrawal—removing money from a bank account; writing a check is a withdrawal

Bodnar, Janet. *Dollars & Sense for Kids: What They Need to Know about Money—and How to Tell Them.* Washington, D. C.: Kiplinger Books, 1999.

Harman, Hollis Page. *Money Sense for Kids!* Hauppauge, New York: Barron's Educational Series, 1999.

Kids, Cash, Plastic and You: A Guidebook for Families on Mastering Money. U. S. Department of Consumer Affairs and MasterCard International.

Mayr, Diane. *The Everything Kids' Money Book: from Saving to Spending to Investing—Learn All about Money!* Holbrook, Massachusetts: Adams Media Corporation, 2000.

Otfinoski, Steven. *Money: Earning It, Saving It, Spending It, Growing It, Sharing It.* New York: Scholastic, 1996.

Automatic Teller
    Machine (ATM), 43, 44

Bentonville, AR, 8, 9
"Bob Levey's Washington," 50

Compound interest, 30–32
Confucius, 11
Credit union, 44, 45

Dryden, John, 16

Emerson, Ralph Waldo, 11
Europe, 39

Federal Deposit Insurance
    Corporation (FDIC), 36
Florence, Italy, 39
Ford, Henry, 16
Franklin, Ben, 11

Great Depression, 8

Hakuta, Ken, 11

Internet, 10
Italy, 39

Lego, 47

Missouri, University of, 9
Mount Vernon, 19

Quinn, Jane Bryant, 16

Rome, 39
Ruskin, John, 16

Singer, Isaac, 57

Wal-Mart, 8, 10
Walton, Sam, 8–10, 12, 17
Walton's, 9
Washington, George, 19
Washington Post, 50

DORIS VALLIANT teaches Advanced Placement English at Easton High School in Easton, Maryland. She writes for regional publications and occasionally does consulting work for the College Board. She budgets, saves, and endeavors to control her credit cards.